STEPHANIDES BROTHERS
GREEK MYTHOL

SERIES A: THE GODS OF OLYMPUS   No. 4

The original Greek edition of this book has been approved by the Hellenic Ministry of Education as a supplementary reader.

THE MYTH OF PERSEPHONE
DEMETER · ARTEMIS

Retold by MENELAOS STEPHANIDES
Illustrated by YANNIS STEPHANIDES

Translation BRUCE WALTER

SIGMA PUBLICATIONS
20, MAVROMIHALI ST., 106 80 ATHENS GREECE, TEL: +30 210 3607667, FAX: +30 210 3638941
www.sigmabooks.gr
e-mail: sigma@sigmabooks.gr

THE MYTH OF PERSEPHONE
1st edition 1974
7th edition revised 2006

Printed by "Fotolio - Typicon", bound by Dedes Dionysis and Co.

Copyright © 2006 Sigma Publications - Menelaos Stephanides - Yannis Stephanides
All rights reserved throughout the world
Published and printed in Greece.
ISBN-13: 978-960-425-018-3
ISBN-10: 960-425-018-9

DEMETER

The story of Demeter begins in the days when the terrible war against the Titans had just come to an end. After the bitterest fighting the world had ever seen, Zeus and the gods of Olympus had toppled the fearsome Titans from their thrones and become the new lords of the earth.

In the aftermath of such a war, the victors were beset with a host of serious problems. The most pressing of these was to save the human race from the hunger which was slowly wiping it out.

Those ten long years of fearful war had ravaged the whole earth. Not a blade of green was left, and those few men who had survived wandered in starving bands, begging the gods for help. Zeus was now the lord of earth and sky, and in his desire to help mankind, he made the goddess Demeter responsible for all the plains and forests in the world. It would be her task to see that the earth bore fruit so that both men and animals should have enough to eat.

The mighty Zeus had made a wise choice. No one loved the green meadows and the placid herds with the same passion as did Demeter – and her greatest love was for mankind. She threw herself into the difficult task with enthusiasm. The meadows were soon carpeted with green, and fruit hung from the boughs. No longer faced with immediate starvation, mankind slowly began to multiply. But this was not enough for the gentle goddess.

THE GODDESS OF AGRICULTURE

AT FIRST MEN LIVED LIKE ANIMALS

In those distant times, man had not yet learned to farm the land. He lived in the forest like a wild creature, struggling against savage beasts and the wildness of nature. His home was a cave or a makeshift shelter of branches and his only food the fruit he picked wild from the trees or the occasional animal he managed to kill in the chase. He and his kind were obliged to wander from place to place, for when there was no food left in one spot they had to search elsewhere for more. Often, however, there was nothing to be found and they were ravaged by hunger. At other times, when out collecting food or hunting, they would run into men of another tribe. Then there was no choice but to give battle: a savage blood-bath to decide who had the right to gather a few wild berries, or to go hunting in that particular part of the forest.

It wounded the goddess to the heart to see man suffer so. Something had to be done. She had to find some way of helping more effectively. The shady woods and the wild meadows were beautiful, but they could not always satisfy man's hunger. His way of life would have to be changed.

Then one day, quite suddenly, as Demeter was sitting on a rock and gazing thoughtfully out over the green plain, a thought flashed into her mind. It was the answer to the problem which had been troubling her for so long.

"Yes, that is what I shall do!" she cried. "I shall teach them to till the soil!" and her face lit up with joy. Demeter's thoughts took wing, and the further they flew, the greater her joy became.

"What wonderful changes this will bring to men's lives. Once they have learned to cultivate the land, they will have fields; once they have fields, they will stop wandering from place to place. They will build houses and villages; they will have shelter, gardens and animals of their own. In time, they will learn arts and letters; they will build splendid cities and... yes! they will no longer need to fight among themselves, for each one will have his own field and his own homeland. What a wonderful chain of events! How much can happen if men learn to till the soil. How happy I am!"

MAN LEARNS TO TILL THE SOIL

The kind goddess had no time to waste. She hastily disguised herself as an ordinary woman, came down to earth and set to work. And a hard task it was. It was by no means easy to make people understand. Time and time again she planted, dug and watered, single-handed, showing people her work and all the time explaining patiently. But what difficulties she faced! There were many who mocked her, people who were really ignorant but thought they knew everything. She was mad, they said. If this was how the gods had made the world, it wasn't likely to change. But the wiser ones watched her carefully. They sensed their lack of knowledge, realised they were learning new skills and threw themselves whole-heartedly into the task.

Their reward was not slow to come. How much more abundant was the harvest

CIVILISATION COMES

now that it came from seed they had sown themselves! How much more satisfaction they gained from a field watered with the sweat of their own brow, its ears of corn bending under their own weight!

It was now quite clear which way was right, and little by little everybody began to cultivate the soil. They gave up wandering through the forest in search of roots and berries. People now started to build houses, gather in villages and tend herds. They learned arts and letters, built cities and embellished them with temples and statues. So, civilisation came – and with it would also have come lasting peace, had not Ares, the bloodthirsty god of war, not continually incited men to battle. Yet now he found his task more difficult, for the new way of life had made men hate war as the greatest curse ever visited upon the world.

Helped by Eirene, the goddess of peace, Demeter stood constantly on the watch to frustrate Ares' attempts to spread war, and there were often times when long periods of peace reigned upon the earth. Civilisation flourished, and Demeter was happy. Yet whenever Ares achieved his aims and war flared up among mankind, she grieved to see the destruction of work that had taken tens or even hundreds or years to achieve.

"True happiness is beyond the reach of gods and men alike. One day all may be well, and the next everything is in ruins." Demeter had often had such gloomy thoughts, but this time a persistent foreboding nagged at her mind as she wandered sadly over the gentle foothills of Olympus. At last, she sat down on a rock looking out over the rich greenery which stretched away before her; but her eyes were vague, and her face troubled. Suddenly, her thoughts flew to her daughter, Persephone, and her anxiety swelled to anguish. Persephone was her only child, and she loved her more dearly than any other creature in the world.

"Some harm has come to her," the goddess cried, springing up as if she had been struck. Immediately, a furious wind began to howl and whistle. Then a heart-rending cry drowned the roar of the wind and pierced Demeter's ears: "Mother, they are tak-

THE LOSS OF PERSEPHONE

ing me away!" – a terrible, despairing cry, reaching Olympus from far away over the mountains and the seas. It was uttered only once, yet a reverberating echo followed it and brought it back again and again. As it passed through gorges and over mountains and mingled with the whistling of the wind, so its note changed. Sometimes it sounded like a shriek and sometimes like a sob, sometimes it re-echoed and at others it sank to a faint whisper. The goddess' head was swimming and her heart ready to burst with anguish. "Mother, they are taking me away!" It was the voice of her only daughter, Persephone.

Had a thousand thunderbolts struck the goddess they would not have shaken her as much as the cry she heard. Nothing could keep her on Olympus a moment longer. She rose like a startled bird and ran in search of her daughter, her feet sometimes resting on dry land, sometimes on the waves.

"Persephone, Persephone!" she shouted. She ran, crying and searching, in all directions, until her footsteps at last brought her to the flowery vale of Nysa. There she found a group of water-nymphs, the beautiful Oceanides, who had been Persephone's best friends. The goddess ran anxiously towards them, but their eyes seemed to hold no good news for her.

"Quickly, good maidens," she cried, "tell me – what has become of my daughter?

DEMETER SEARCHES FOR PERSEPHONE

Who has snatched her away?"

"Unhappy goddess," came the reply, "we know nothing; we only heard her cry. She was here with us gathering flowers. Look, here are our baskets. We didn't realise that she had wandered away from us. Then we heard a cry – and that was all."

Demeter did not wait to hear any more. With tears streaming down her face, she ran off to continue her search. For nine days and nine nights she went on looking, but all was in vain; whoever she asked, simple mortal or mighty seer, the answer was the same. They knew nothing.

On the evening of the tenth day, when the new moon rose into the sky, Hecate the moon-goddess appeared before Demeter and said: "I have seen your suffering and I have come to help you. Since nobody else knows anything of your daughter, let me take you to Helios, the god of the sun, for he alone among gods and mortals can have seen your daughter snatched away."

The two goddesses soon reached the golden courts of the sun, and stood dazzled before the great god of the day.

IN THE COURTS OF THE SUN

When the sun saw Demeter, he knew why she had come. "Dear goddess," he said, "I share your sorrow at the misfortune which has befallen you. What has happened to Persephone, however, was the will of her father, Zeus. He gave her to Pluto, lord of Hades, to be his bride. She is now in the Kingdom of the Underworld, and will never again see the light of day."

When Demeter heard these words, her face turned pale as wax and floods of tears gushed from her eyes, but the sun had more to tell: "Persephone was playing and gathering flowers with her friends, the Oceanides, in the flowery vale of Nysa. It was a beautiful spot, with its green trees and sweet-smelling blooms, its warbling birds and laughing waters. Drunk with the beauty of it all, Persephone flitted like a butterfly from flower to flower, not realising how far behind she had left her friends. But while she was delighting in the beauty of the spot, without a care in the world, Pluto, the lord of Hades, was lying in wait nearby, hidden in a crack in the earth. Suddenly, Persephone caught sight of a lovely narcissus, whose petals were just opening. She picked it and held it to her face to smell its delicate fragrance. Persephone had always been a lovely girl, but in that moment she was lovelier than ever. Pluto, who had watched the whole scene, could restrain himself no longer. With a single blow he split the earth asunder and lunged forward into the daylight upon his golden chariot, drawn by the immortal, coal-black horses of Hades. In a flash, he had dragged Persephone up beside him. She scarcely had time to sob, "mother, they are taking me away," before the horses

THE AWFUL TRUTH

plunged back into the dark earth, blinded by the light of day.

The sun god saw that as his tale unfolded, so Demeter's misery deepened. He tried to comfort her. "Do not grieve," he said, "Pluto is a great lord, and the Kingdom of the Underworld is boundless, for the dead far outnumber the living. Your daughter will live in courts of gold and countless shades of the dead will honour and worship her just as they worship the immortal Pluto, brother of almighty Zeus, who numbers you among his sisters."

But these words only increased Demeter's grief, for she saw that she had lost all that was dearest to her in the world – her only daughter.

A MOTHER'S GRIEF

Everything was clear to her now, and the pain of her knowledge ruined not only her life but all the beauty she had created. Now, nothing would grow on earth and a frozen north wind raged, stripping the dying leaves from the trees and whirling them through the air. Gone were the lovely flowers and the green grass. Gone were the rich ears and the sweet fruit. Nothing was left. People, animals and birds began to grow hungry and cold and many of them died. Cries of mourning could be heard on all sides. Everybody begged Demeter to make the earth green again, to make the trees bear fruit and to bring a smile back to the face of the world, but Demeter's grief was so deep that it made her deaf to all cries and blind to all tragedies but her own.

She was so angry with Zeus for giving their daughter to Pluto without considering her maternal feelings that she never wanted to see Olympus again. Like a mortal mother sorrowing for her lost one, she stumbled blindly over the face of the earth crying and wailing. In the course of her wanderings, she eventually arrived before the gates of Eleusis. In that spot there stands a well –'the well of the maidens'– which still exists today. Exhausted, Demeter drank a little water and then sat down upon a large stone, which has been called 'the wailing stone' ever since. The goddess had been sitting there for some hours, buried in her grief, when she was found by four girls who had come for water. They were filled with pity at the sight of this weeping woman in black, and they asked her who she was and what they could do to help her.

"My name is Dio," Demeter replied, not wishing to reveal her true identity. "I come from Crete and I was carried away by pirates, but I managed to escape them, and since then I have been wandering from place to place. Now, I have no idea where I am. If you are from a rich and kind family, as you seem to be, I am good at many kinds of work. I know how to bring up children, how to care for the aged and how to set the serving-girls their various tasks."

"We are the daughters of Celeus, king of Eleusis," the eldest of the girls replied. "Come with us, and we shall take you to our mother, Queen Metaneira. She needs a

THE WAILING STONE

IAMBE AND HER TRICKS

sensible woman to look after our baby brother, little Demophon." And so they took the stranger to the palace.

As soon as Demeter crossed the threshold, however, the whole palace was flooded with divine light. An astonished Metaneira rose to greet the visitor and to offer her royal throne, for she realised that this was no ordinary mortal. Demeter, however, refused to be seated and remained sadly standing there until Iambe, the queen's hand-maiden, brought a stool for her. Seeing Demeter's sad face, Iambe began to tell jokes to try and make her laugh. She made such funny faces and so many amusing gestures that a smile finally appeared on Demeter's lips and she accepted a cup of wine. For the first time since the loss of her daughter Persephone, a little happiness had come into her heart.

Demeter stayed at the palace of Celeus, and Metaneira gave the goddess her newly-born son Demophon to nurse. Wishing to reward the royal couple for the kindness they had shown her, Demeter decided to make the baby immortal. First she took the child into her arms and breathed her divine breath into his lungs, then she anointed his body with ambrosia and secretly placed him in a lighted furnace at night, to make his body everlasting. Unluckily, Metaneira saw her doing this, and thinking that Demeter had gone mad she let out such screams that she alarmed the goddess, who took the baby out of the oven and gave it back to the queen saying: "Take your child and look after him yourself from now on. I had hoped to make him into a being that would never know old age and death, and would be honoured for ever. Know that I am the goddess Demeter, and that I wished to thank you for all that you have done for me."

As soon as Demeter revealed her identity, the same divine light again flooded the palace, and the goddess once more appeared in all her former glory. Metaneira and Celeus knelt before her and Demeter commanded the king to build her a

DEMETER REVEALS HERSELF

temple near the spring of Callirrhoe, at Eleusis. And there, far from Olympus, the unhappy goddess made her home.

In the meantime, however, the earth had become a desert where both men and animals were dying of starvation. Only around Eleusis could a little greenery still be found and it was feared that this, too, would disappear.

THE RETURN OF SPRING

Zeus saw all this and realised that he must do something to repair the harm which had been done. So he sent Hermes to bring Persephone back – but only after he had given her some pomegranate seeds to eat so that she would not forget her husband. And so from that time onwards Persephone has spent one half of the year with her mother and the other half with Pluto in the Kingdom of the Underworld. Ever since then, in spring and summer the mountains and the plains are clothed in green and the earth garlanded with flowers. All nature rejoices, for these are the seasons when Persephone is at her mother's side; and Demeter, too, in her joy sees to it that the earth is both lovely and fertile. But when Persephone leaves, then the autumn comes, and the cold winter. The leaves fall from the trees and all is miserable and gloomy, for Demeter, too, is sad that her only daughter is far from the light of day, in the inky blackness of Hades. And so it has continued: every spring Demeter welcomes her beloved daughter back, and in her happiness throws herself into her favourite task, trying to sweeten the painful life of man.

However, not everybody had yet learned how to cultivate the earth. In distant parts of the world men still lived like savages, just as in the old days.

This was how people lived in Scythia, which was then ruled by King Lyngus. Demeter decided to send a hero there, a man who would scorn all dangers in his efforts to teach men the agriculture which would bring them civilisation. The man best fitted for the task, she felt, was Triptolemus, the eldest son of King Celeus. Demeter gave her hero a winged chariot and two dragons to shield him from evil powers, and he set out for distant Scythia. His strongest protection, however, was his own brave heart. This fearless hero faced many terrible dangers, but he overcame them all with his sword and finally taught the Scythians how to cultivate the soil. Thus peace slowly came to that people and their land.

TRIPTOLEMUS IN SCYTHIA

King Lyngus, however, was far from satisfied. He was jealous of Triptolemus and made up his mind to kill him and then spread the word that it was he, Lyngus, who had brought the art of agriculture to his people. But how was he to rid himself of Triptolemus, who killed everybody sent to murder him? Finally, he decided to do the deed himself. Since he did not want to meet the same fate as the others, he decided to commit the crime while Triptolemus was sleeping – yet how could he do so when the hero was guarded in his sleep by the winged dragons Demeter had given him?

In the end, he hit upon a devilish plan. He invited Triptolemus to his palace and served him a splendid feast accompanied by choice wines. He thanked him for the great services he had performed for Scythia and then led him into one of the chambers of the palace to sleep.

Late that night, while Triptolemus was slumbering deeply, Lyngus crept into his room clutching a sharp-pointed dagger. "Ha! The plan has worked!" said Lyngus to himself, but at the very moment when he was raising the dagger, he felt his wrist caught in a vice-like grip. The knife fell to the ground. The terrified Lyngus turned his head and found himself face to face with the goddess Demeter.

"Lyngus, you have sealed your own fate," the goddess hissed. "A swine you are and a swine you shall remain for ever. And immediately the king was transformed into a wild boar which fled panic-stricken into the forest, while Triptolemus left Scythia unharmed, to bring Demeter's gift of agriculture to the other backward peoples of the world. From then on, woe betide anyone who dared to lay a finger on the goddess' fearless favourite.

Demeter's task was a sacred one, and all who tried to frustrate or destroy her work had to be punished severely; but the harshest punishment of all was dealt to Erysichthon, the king of Thessaly, the man who wantonly cut down trees.

This, too, is a myth of course, but a very useful

one. Forests were no less valuable to man in those days than they are today. It was an evil deed to cut down a tree, for people believed that in every tree there dwelt a nymph, called a dryad – and that dryad would live only as long as the tree itself. Whoever wished to cut a tree down had to think very seriously before he did so, for Demeter loved and protected the dryads. There was not a man in Greece who did not know this and Erysichthon, being a king, should certainly have known the wishes of the gods even better than an ordinary man. Yet while he should have tried to save the forests, his craving for luxury blinded him to his duty and he cut down trees pitilessly, merely to build himself a new palace. He went beyond all bounds, however, when his eye fell upon a hundred-year old oak which stood at the entrance to the sacred grove.

When the king arrived with his courtiers before the sacred tree, the whole group stood silent and hesitant. Finally, the eldest of them came forward and said to the king, "Your Majesty, haven't you done enough damage to the forest, building this new palace of yours? Wasn't your old palace beautiful enough? Listen to a word of advice: beauty is something which everyone admires; luxury is not. Try to understand that, and don't cut down the tree. For your own sake, pity the dryad that lives there, for Demeter..."

But Erysichthon cut him short: "Keep your advice to yourself, old man, and don't think your white hair will protect you. What do I care about dryads or about Demeter? I am protected by stronger gods. Even if Demeter herself lived in this oak tree, I would still cut it down!" With these words, he seized an axe from a slave and furiously began chopping at the noble oak. Immediately he did so, a miracle occurred. Blood spurted from the wounded trunk! The onlookers were horrified, and a slave tried to hold the king back. Erysichthon turned on the man in fury and killed him, shouting:

**ERYSICHTHON
MURDERER OF TREES**

"There, you dog, I'll teach you to warn me about Demeter!" And with these words he renewed his attack upon the tree until it toppled beneath his blows and the dryad in it died.

Now, that dryad had been more dearly loved than any other in the grove, and her sisters ran in tears to Demeter and told her of the terrible thing which had happened.

"See what he did, the beast," they cried, "and hear what he said about you, mighty goddess! – 'Even if Demeter herself lived in that oak I would still cut it down,' he snarled – and, 'You dog, I'll teach you to warn me about Demeter!' – and then he killed the poor slave and cut down the tree and we lost the best friend we had."

HUNGER VISITS ERYSICHTHON

The goddess was furious when she heard these words, and immediately thought of a punishment to fit the hideous crime. Now it was the turn of Erysichthon to be pitied – if such men can be said to deserve any pity. This is how he was punished.

Demeter ordered a dryad to go to the distant Caucasus and seek out Peina, the goddess of hunger. The dryad was to tell her that by Demeter's command she should go to Erysichthon and breathe her affliction into his body.

In an instant, the dryad had reached the Caucasus and found the goddess of hunger in a cave on a dry, thorny mountainside. Hunger was bony, haggard and tousle-haired. Her robe was black, and her eyes were sunk deep in their sockets. The dryad recoiled in horror when she saw her, but she soon got her courage back and told her why she had come to the Caucasus.

The goddess of hunger obeyed Demeter's command upon the instant, and carried by a whirlwind, she soon reached the palace of Erysichthon. Night had long since fallen and she found him fast asleep. Hunger covered him with her wings and breathed her poisoned breath upon his face. That was all. Immediately afterwards she disappeared at the same wild speed with which she had come.

And then something strange happened. Although Erysichthon was still fast asleep, his jaws began to open and close because he could see food in his sleep; and although there was nothing in his mouth, he started chewing and swallowing. Suddenly the king woke up, hunger gnawing at his entrails. He roused his servants immediately and bellowed at them to scour the land, drag the seas and empty the skies, and to place whatever they could find to eat before him. He gulped food down without pausing for breath, yet the more he ate, the more he complained of his hunger. His slaves brought him dish after dish spilling over with food and all the while he shouted that it was too little and sent them back for more. Food that would have sufficed to feed whole nations was not enough to fill his stomach. The harder he chewed and swallowed, the sharper his hunger grew. His stomach was like a bottomless pit: the more he tried to fill it, the emptier it seemed; insatiable pangs of hunger tore at his entrails and tortured him all the more. And so his whole fortune disappeared into his stomach without being able to quench the fires that burned there. Finally, when he had gobbled up all his wealth, lost his kingdom and his followers and sold his last slave, he found himself left with nothing but his daughter, Mistra, who pitied him although she

THE AWFUL PANGS

ERYSICHTHON SELLS HIS DAUGHTER

surely deserved a better father.

This Mistra was so beautiful that the sea-god himself, Poseidon, had once fallen in love with her. Now her father, unable to resist his appetite, sold her too. While on her way to slavery, however, Mistra begged Poseidon for his help, and the sea-god, who still loved her, bestowed on her the power to change herself into any form she wished. So Mistra became a bird and immediately flew back to her father. And he sold her again. She became a horse and returned once more. And again he sold her. And so she became a heifer, and then a doe and so it went on until finally, having changed herself into a roe-deer, she found herself faced by a flood-swollen river which she could not cross. Then Erysichthon could no longer control himself. He fell ravenously upon his own flesh and died in horrible agony.

Thus died the man who killed trees; and thus Demeter protected her good works from a few evil men, by showing that hunger awaits those who destroy her woodlands. Most people, however, loved the trees and the green plains. They loved their work on the land and honoured the goddess Demeter at great festivals. One of these was the Eleusinian Mysteries, which was among the greatest feasts of the year. This festival, which took place every spring, was a gay celebration at which men honoured Demeter and welcomed the return of her daughter Persephone before throwing themselves into the year's work in the fields, as the goddess of agriculture had taught them.

ARTEMIS

In the far distant past, on nights when Zeus had retired to rest and the full moon shone bright in the starry sky, a happy party of beautiful nereids would wander through the woods. A tall, lithe maiden stood out amongst them, the most beautiful of them all. All the others obeyed her, and when the group made merry in some clearing in the woods she always proved herself the finest singer and dancer. Her name was Artemis; she was the goddess of moonlit nights and the great queen of the forests. She wore a short smock which emphasised the divine grace of her body, and when the silvery beams of the moon fell upon her, she radiated mythical beauty and imposing dignity. She loved hunting and often carried a gilded bow, while from her shoulder hung a golden quiver, filled with arrows which always shot true.

A PROUD GODDESS

Artemis was the daughter of the mighty Zeus and of the goddess Leto. She was the twin sister of golden-haired Apollo, and in an earlier chapter we saw what sufferings Leto went through before she bore her two children. Artemis loved her mother and the other gods of Olympus. She was bold and proud, and woe betide any who slighted her or any other goddess. When, in spite of this, the two giant Aloades once dared to insult her, Artemis scorned their mighty strength and gave them the punishment they deserved.

Otus and Ephialtes, as they were called, were the two sons of the giant Aloeus. Every year, they grew one fathom in height and one cubit in width. As their size in-

THE PUNISHMENT OF THE TWO ALOADES

creased, so did their strength – and not only their strength, but their insolence. Mere mortals were of no consequence to them, and these they killed simply for pleasure. Finally, however, they became so bold that they even began to threaten the gods of Olympus. "Wait till we have grown a little taller," they said, "and we shall pile Mount Pelion on Mount Ossa and reach to the very heavens themselves – and then we shall snatch Hera and Artemis away from you!"

The gods certainly had cause to fear this pair. For had they not chained Ares, the fearsome god of war, and kept him hidden away for thirteen months? What troubled the gods even more was that these two giants had been born virtually immortal, and neither god nor man could kill them. Fate had decreed that they would die only if the one killed the other. Yet how could such an end overtake the two Aloades, whose ambitions bound them together even more firmly than the brotherly blood which flowed in their veins?

Artemis, however, had laid her plans. One day, when the two Aloades went out hunting, the goddess trailed them. The two giants were lying in ambush near each other, waiting for a deer to cross their path. The goddess caught a doe and then released it in a spot where it would pass directly between the two brothers. As soon as Otus and Ephialtes saw the doe, they both took aim immediately. They bent back their bows with all their strength and loosed their shafts like lightning-bolts. The goddess, however, made sure that they missed the doe, and since the target they were aiming at lay exactly between them, their arrows drove home full force into each other's foreheads. Artemis' plan had succeeded: the two Aloades fell dead. There was indescribable joy when the news of the terrible giants' end became known, and everybody sang hymns of praise to Artemis in honour of her great achievement.

In Greece, Artemis was also widely worshipped as the goddess of chastity, and along with her they honoured Hippolytus, a handsome young man who dedicated his life to the service of the goddess and by his death became the symbol of upright and honourable youth.

HIPPOLYTUS FOLLOWS ARTEMIS

Hippolytus was the son of the hero Theseus, king of Athens. His mother was the lovely Antiope, queen of the Amazons, who fell at Theseus' side fighting bravely in the defence of Athens. Theseus later remarried; his second wife was Phaedra, daughter of the king of Crete, Minos. After the king's second marriage, Hippolytus left Athens and went to the Peloponnese where he stayed with his great-grandfather, the sage Pittheus. Pittheus, who was king of Troezen, made the young man heir to his throne.

Hippolytus had inherited two qualities from his Amazonian mother: a love of horses and a deep-rooted adoration for the goddess Artemis. Four splendid steeds drew his chariot, which he controlled with breath-taking skill. He took part in the Olympic games, and when he returned victorious to Troezen, standing upright upon his chariot, the young people of the town ran to greet him as if he were a god from Olympus.

Yet far more important in the young man's life was his worship of the goddess Artemis as the symbol of the purity of youth. He spent the greater part of his time in the goddess' sacred grove, and he had become the dearest person in the world to her. The son of Theseus was the only mortal the goddess would meet and speak with. Together they hunted deer and wild boar, together they drank crystal-clear water from shady springs and together they rode in company, side by side. Artemis' love for Hippolytus was deep, chaste and sisterly, and his love for the goddess was filled with respect, worship and purity.

However, Aphrodite, the goddess of love, felt insulted by the fervour Hippolytus showed in his worship of Artemis. She could not bear to see him pass her statue without even stopping to beg a favour or to lay an offering at her feet.

"What right," she cried, "has he to ride at her side day after day? Mortals were created to worship all the gods of Olympus, and not just one alone!" And with these words, she waited for her chance to strike.

HIPPOLYTUS AND PHAEDRA

Now one day, Hippolytus went to Athens to attend a religious ceremony at his father's palace. Aphrodite knew that there he would meet his step-mother, Phaedra, and that this woman would be the most suitable person to use as a tool to bring about the young man's destruction. One shaft from the bow of her winged son, Eros, was all Aphrodite needed to make Phaedra forget her love for her husband and feel passionate longing for the noble youth. Sure enough, when the queen of Athens set eyes upon the lithe young figure of Hippolytus, her heart beat faster. Alarmed by her feelings, she tried to bring herself to her senses and think of the harm she would do to her husband, but it was impossible to listen to the voice of reason. The most she could do was to prevent herself from speaking to Hippolytus.

Once the young man had left, Phaedra could find no peace. She was unable to sleep or eat and became thin and pale. One day, impatient to see Hippolytus again, she went to Troezen. There, she hid in the temple of Aphrodite or 'The Temple of the Secret Watcher' as it has been called ever since. From her hiding-place, she could see the young man in the distance as he performed gymnastics, but she dared not show herself, and returned to Athens as secretly as she had come.

A few days later, the great feast of the Pan-Athenian procession took place, and Hippolytus, Phaedra and Theseus found themselves in Athens once more. Throughout the festival, Phaedra felt her heart beating wildly, for the young man was standing close beside her. When the ceremonies were over, she hurried straight up to the palace, hoping that there she might find some peace of mind, but as soon as she reached the terrace, she found her eyes sweeping the crowd for a glimpse of the fair young man. While she was watching, a splendid black horse was led forward. It was unbroken, and no-one had yet succeeded in mounting its back. With brilliant skill, Hippolytus seized the horse by its halter and bounded athwart its flanks. The creature responded to its rider's will instantly and reared upwards superbly upon its hind legs, whilst all the onlookers marvelled at the handsome and courageous young man who had tamed the proud stallion.

With bated breath Phaedra followed the scene from the palace walls, and when everything was over and she found Hippolytus alone, she decided that she must unburden herself once and for all.

"Stay in Athens, Hippolytus," she begged him. "I don't want Theseus any longer. It was he who abandoned my sister Ariadne on Naxos. It was because of him that your mother was killed. He may even kill me. You must take revenge, Hippolytus. The goddess Aphrodite is on our side. Become king of Athens, and I will be your devoted wife and queen."

How little Phaedra knew of Hippolytus! How could such a sick idea find a place in a heart as pure as his? Betray his father, the renowned hero Theseus, whom even the gods admired for his brave and noble deeds? Betray Artemis, the eagle-eyed huntress to whom he had dedicated his life? As if he could perform such a deed!

Hippolytus fixed Phaedra with a gaze of such cold contempt that her heart quailed. And then he hurled the words in her face: "Never! Shame on you!"

With a strangled cry of despair, Phaedra buried her face in her hands and ran to hide herself in the next room, whilst Hippolytus stood thinking only of his father and pitying him with all the power of his soul.

"Great Zeus," he swore at last, "I give my oath that I shall never tell my father what I know. Let her see for herself the injury she was ready to do him."

Phaedra realised, of course, what a terrible thing she had done, but she lacked the will to undo the harm. The one evil deed pushed her on to another, three times more terrible.

"Never! Shame on you!" She echoed his stinging words; "But if I am lost, then you shall be dragged down with me!" Then she tore her clothes, dug her nails into her arms and neck, threw her hair into disorder and burst from the room.

"Help, help!" she cried, and in broken phrases, punctuated by sobs, she laid the blame on the innocent youth. She then shut herself in her room once more and wrote a letter to Theseus, treacherously accusing Hippolytus of the crime she had herself committed. Then, pinning the note to her robe, she hanged herself from the crossbeam of the door and brought her life to a miserable close.

THESEUS CASTS OUT HIPPOLYTUS

The frightful news soon reached Theseus. When he saw his wife's body and read the letter, he stood as if transfixed. He could not bring himself to believe the sight before him and the words he read. Yet his wife was dead and how else but through the treacherous lust of his son Hippolytus?

"How could I have been so blind," he cried. "Turn him out and let him never again set foot in Athens!"

At that moment, Hippolytus appeared. "You are making a terrible mistake, father," he said, "I am not guilty."

"You hypocrite! You swore a vow of chastity to the goddess Artemis and now you betray her, your father and your step-mother. It was you who killed her, murderer! Get out! Get out and never set eyes on me again!"

Hippolytus did not wish to speak out, for he had sworn never to lay the blame on Phaedra. For this reason, he decided to swear a solemn oath.

"Listen, father. I swear to Zeus that I will disappear without name or glory, without motherland and without home, pursued by gods and men, if I am evil; and when I die, may my body lie unburied, my bones picked clean by birds of prey. I can say no more."

"Oh, ye gods, what a shameless liar. There's the body, there's the letter. Everything betrays you, ungrateful beast. Leave! I cannot bear the sight of you!"

And rather than reveal the truth, Hippolytus chose to leave. He ran straight to his horses, harnessed them to the chariot, and seizing the reins galloped off down the road towards the Peloponnese.

As soon as he had left, Theseus' anger overflowed: "Oh, father Poseidon, ruler of the seas," he cried, "you promised me three wishes and now I beg for one of them. Do not let Hippolytus reach Troezen."

A FATHER'S CURSE

Why, Theseus, why? Why did you act in haste? Why did you not look more closely? Why did you not turn to others for advice, instead of acting in the heat of the moment? Blinded by your wrath, you took the rash decision and hurled the curse which brought death upon your son! And as for you, unlucky Hippolytus, your fate is sealed. You will never again ride victorious into Troezen, and the longing maidens will set eyes on you no more. You will never again run at Artemis' side in the cool meadows, and never so much as offer another rose to the goddess you adored, for now death lies in wait for you upon your road!

Unaware of the fate which awaited him, Hippolytus was now skirting the Scironian

THE DEATH OF HIPPOLYTUS

Rocks, speeding along the rough and narrow road that leads to Corinth between the mountain and the sea. Though his heart was bursting with grief, he guided his chariot with a sure hand over the winding, rock-strewn way. Then, all of a sudden, a huge wave disgorged upon the shore a monstrous bull which bellowed hideously and snorted water from its nostrils. The startled horses bolted and dragged the chariot toward the cliff's edge. Had anyone but Hippolytus been at the reins, they would have tumbled headlong to the rocky shore below. But there was not a charioteer in the world who could match Hippolytus. Heaving upon the reins, he arched his body back like an oarsman and achieved the impossible feat of forcing the bolting horses back upon the road. Pursued by the roaring bull, the horses dragged the chariot along at breakneck speed. Yet Hippolytus held them on their course, avoiding death by a hairsbreadth at every instant. In no time they had left the Scironian Rocks behind them and were galloping madly towards the Isthmus of Corinth with the bull still in pursuit. And here the end came. Although Poseidon's monster had failed to dash Hippolytus against the rocks, an old, gnarled olive-tree proved the final cause of his disaster. A harness-belt streaming in the wind caught on a dry branch and in a second all was over. The horses were hurled into the air, the sturdy chariot was dashed to pieces against the boulders and Hippolytus, tangled in the reins, was dashed over the stones and wounded mortally. As he lay dying, the goddess Artemis appeared upon her chariot, bringing with her his father, Theseus. With an aching heart, the goddess revealed the whole story to the king of Athens, who now knelt weeping at his son's side.

Then the noble youth gathered what strength was left to him, raised his head a little and said: "Do not cry, father, it was not your fault if you were deceived. I shall love you, even from the underworld." And those were his last words.

When he died, Artemis took the youth and buried him in that same grove at Troezen where he had first set eyes upon the goddess.

Heartbroken at the death of his son, and at the great and irreparable wrong he had done him, Theseus came to the sacred grove and marked out the spot where a temple would stand. Soon, a simple but beautiful temple rose at the side of Hippolytus' grave. Here the young man was worshipped as a god, and all the young men and maidens of Troezen brought a lock of their hair before their wedding and offered it to the son of Theseus who had been so unjustly sacrificed. This gesture showed that they would go pure and untouched to their marriage vows. Thus Hippolytus continued to live on in the memory of the people of Troezen. Indeed, they never admitted that he had died. "How is it possible," they argued, "for Hippolytus to have been killed by his horses? No, the horses didn't kill Hippolytus. He lives. Artemis has taken him up into the sky and placed him among the stars." They showed his grave to no-one. But at night, they would point to a constellation in the sky and say: "There he is." And from that day onwards, the constellation has been called Iniochus, the Charioteer.

INIOCHUS THE CHARIOTEER

And now here is another myth in which a fair young man again suffers an undeserved death. And if in the previous myth we saw that the unjust fate of Hippolytus was the will of the goddess Aphrodite, in this we shall see how Artemis herself behaved cruelly.

From as far back as the age of the fearsome Cronus, a law had existed that any man who set eyes upon a god unless the god himself wished it, must surely die. It was an unjust law, and one which Artemis applied with unnecessary harshness in the case of Actaeon, who unintentionally chanced to catch sight of the goddess while she was bathing.

It happened on a hot summer's day. Artemis was with a party of nymphs and nereids of the forest. Faint with the heat, they longed to take a bathe to cool themselves. Artemis, however, never bathed in sea or river, lake or spring, because she feared that some indiscreet eye might fall upon her. Up to this moment, indeed, neither god nor man had ever seen the goddess bathing. So Artemis went with her friends to cool herself in the still waters of a cave, buried high up on the thickly-wooded slopes of Mount Cithaeron. The whole group left their clothes on the rocks and jumped into the crystal-clear waters with happy shouts. Artemis jumped first, and she played and frolicked in the water as if she were a little child. The nymphs and nereids followed her and they all played and laughed together, happy and carefree.

ACTAEON GLIMPSES ARTEMIS

At the same time, a party of hunters happened to be passing by. Among them was Actaeon, the handsome crown prince of Thebes. He had gone on ahead of the others, and, as he was thirsty, was looking for water. Suddenly, he saw the entrance to a cave. It was the cave where Artemis was. Leaving his dogs outside, the prince went in to look for water. After he had gone forward a few steps, he heard the sound of splashing, and paused thoughtfully.

"No, Actaeon, don't go on," a voice inside him seemed to say. "Remember the law of Cronus. Who knows who may be in the cave?"

Yet Actaeon did go on, and suddenly, rounding a bend in the rock, he came face to face with the party of goddesses.

At that moment, the lovely Artemis was rising from the water. Her lithe body glowed in the half-light of the cave with an indescribable, divine beauty which no man's eyes had ever yet beheld.

It was two nymphs who first saw Actaeon, and a cry of alarm escaped them. Artemis turned to see what had happened and saw Actaeon standing a little further off. She blushed from head to foot in her shame and rage and became more lovely still. The nymphs rushed to shield her from Actaeon's eyes, but the harm had been done. Artemis was so outraged that Actaeon's doom was sealed. The goddess transformed the hapless youth into a deer.

Now a deer, Actaeon ran to escape, but when he emerged from the cave, his own dogs began to hunt him down. Actaeon struggled to speak, to tell his dogs not to harm him, to let them know that the deer they were hunting was their own beloved master. But he no longer had the power of speech, and they bore down on him and sank their fangs into his throat – and the tragic irony of it was that the dogs then went searching for Actaeon to show him their rich prize. When the other hunters realised that Actaeon was missing, they too went in search of their friend. In the evening, tired and with all hope lost, they slung the slain deer over the back of a horse and took the road back for Thebes. How could any of them imagine that the deer was Actaeon himself, alone among gods and men to have seen Artemis in her nakedness?

ACTAEON'S CRUEL FATE

The punishments of Artemis were harsh, and for that reason people were careful to behave as the goddess wished.

THE BEAR CHILDREN OF VRAVRON

At Vravron, in Attica, there was a great festival every five years, which had its origin in the following incident: a tame bear used to wander at liberty in the streets of Athens and all the inhabitants thought of it as a holy animal, protected by Artemis. The Athenians, who loved the beast, fed and took care of it. The bear was the children's best friend. They played with it and teased it without its ever losing its temper or doing any of them any harm. One day, however, a little girl got so carried away with her teasing that she kicked the bear and pinched it and finally took a stick and started beating the creature wherever she could find a target. Then the animal finally lost its temper, lunged at the girl and squeezed her to death in its grip.

When the little girl's brothers heard the terrible news, without pausing to think, they went and killed the bear – killed, that is, the sacred animal protected by Artemis. After that, a great misery hung over Athens. A terrible disease struck down the children of Attica.

Then the Athenians sent messengers to seek the advice of the oracle and were told that they must dedicate their daughters to Artemis in the guise of a bear. This was the beginning of the Vravronia, a beautiful ceremony which took place every five years, when the Athenians dressed all their daughters between five and ten in costumes the colour of bear-skins and walked with them in a long procession to the temple of Artemis at Vravron. There, they sacrificed a she-goat or a calf to the goddess, and the priestesses blessed the 'bear girls' as they were called. They then went off to play, and the little plain of Vravron seemed quite changed from its usual self as it filled with the little 'bear girls' running, jumping and dancing with happy cries over the fresh, green turf.

It was only with a great deal of effort that their parents were able to round them up again so they could set off early, for it was a long walk back to Athens.

WITH OUR YOUNG READERS IN MIND

This mythology was written with the intention of providing children with reading material which would be instructive and educational, but at the same time capable of instilling a love for good books and drawing the child away from the shallow, though often superficially attractive content of some children's readers.

To achieve this aim, an approach was needed which would bring the myth to life without departing from its original, ancient form.

We believe that illustrations of high quality go a long way towards achieving such an aim. We have used them freely, in the belief that they will not only encourage the child to read the text, but will lead to a more vivid understanding of the myth itself, and leave a lasting impression on the mind.

Special care was needed in the handling of the text. For mythology to make attractive reading must naturally rely on the author's ability, and certainly we have done what was within our power; but for the book to have educational value it must be based on sound principles. It is on this aspect of our work that we should like to dwell.

In the first place, we reject the assumption that Greek mythology is unsuitable for children. Unlike others, we find that it contains a superabundance of educationally valuable myths. Neither do we consider as undesirable those myths which present the gods as unjust in their dealings. The ancients took their gods and formed them from the stuff of everyday reality. And reality, in those harsh times, was more often unjust than not. It would, of course, have been undesirable if we had attempted to paint those unjust deeds in favourable colours, and that is precisely what we have avoided doing. Nor do we believe that a myth deserves a place in the body of Greek mythology simply because it happens to have survived. Works which have achieved immortality thanks to poets of Homeric stature bear no relation at all to those worthless and ribald myths which were concocted with the obvious aim of justifying the conduct of certain people in high places.

It was with these points in mind that we embarked on the task of making our choice among the myths in all their wide variety of differing versions. By rejecting that barren and prudish approach which runs counter to modern educational principles, we found that all the more significant myths fitted comfortably into our scheme. However, we found that broad-mindedness alone was not enough: the whole work had to aim at promoting and exploiting the abundance of positive features to be found in Greek mythology without its falling into a didactic or preaching tone.

This is not to say that we consider our work to be a new departure, however much so it may seem to many. We have, in fact, done nothing more than follow the example of the great tragedians of ancient times. Choosing, as they did, our material from Greek mythology we have, like them, portrayed moral values which hold good the world over. We could see no other way of proceeding, and all the more so since we have written our mythology with the young reader in mind.